Mental Well-Being and Digestive Process

The Digestive System's Impact on Mental Wellness

BY

Dave F. Lange

INTRODUCTION

Today's fast-paced world of processed meals, stress, and sedentary lifestyles makes the relationship between gut health and mental health more important than it has ever been. This book, "Digestion and Mental Health," sets out to investigate the complex connection between our eating habits and our emotional states. It explores the relationship between the stomach and the brain, how it affects our mental health, and how taking care of our digestive systems may result in a happier, more balanced existence. In these pages, we will explore the world of gut bacteria as well as the complex network of neurons that line our intestines and their tremendous impact on our emotions and cognitive processes. This book is your guide to reaching a state of harmony where a healthy stomach translates into a better mind, including everything from the most recent scientific findings to useful food and lifestyle recommendations. Come explore the intriguing relationship between mental health and digestion and learn how to take control of your health from the inside out.

CHAPTER ONE

THE MICROBIOME GUT:

Helping people feel happy and calm.

Your stomach, intestines, and colon are all parts of your gastrointestinal system, or "gut." It excretes trash while digesting and absorbing nutrients from meals. Gut health isn't well defined, and it might imply various things to academics, doctors, and members of the public. Gut health is defined on this page as having a balanced gut flora and few digestive complaints. Your large intestine is home to over 200 different types of bacteria, viruses, and fungi. Your gut microbiome is made up of the bacteria and other microbes there. Food is broken down by bacteria so that your body can utilize the nutrients. Some disorders may be caused by specific gut bacterial species. A healthy body requires a variety of microbes, many of which are helpful to human health. We are discovering that a key determinant of the health of your microbiome is the diversity of bacteria in your gut. Your physical and emotional health may be affected by the condition of your stomach. The kind of bacteria in your digestive system might change depending on a variety of variables, including the foods you consume. Both immediate and long-term impacts on the ecosystem of our gut microbiota may result from what we consume. A complex community of bacteria called the gut microbiome, often known as "the microbiome gut," lives in the human gastrointestinal tract, particularly in the intestines. Numerous different microorganisms, such as bacteria, viruses, fungi, and other single-celled creatures, make up this microbial ecosystem. It contributes significantly to many facets of human health and creates a dynamic, linked ecosystem inside the digestive system. The collection of microbes living in the gut, known as the gut microbiome, varies from person to person depending on things including genetics, nutrition, environment, and early experiences. These microbes have complex interactions with the human body, the immune system, metabolism, and even elements of digestion and mental health. The gut microbiome is a topic of continuing scientific investigation and discovery as a result of studies into its significant influence on human health. It is becoming more clear that maintaining a healthy gut microbiota is essential for general health and well-being.

Mood, particularly sensations of pleasure and serenity, and the gut microbiota are related in an intriguing and young field of study. The gut microbiome may affect a person's mental and emotional health in several ways, while the precise processes are currently under investigation.

First, is neurotransmitter synthesis Neurotransmitters are chemical messengers that play a critical role in controlling mood, and certain gut bacteria can create them. For instance, certain bacteria may create serotonin, a neurotransmitter well-known for fostering emotions of pleasure and well-being. When these bacteria are numerous and working well, they may help the gut produce more serotonin, which may affect mood.

Secondly, immunity and inflammation The body's immune system and inflammatory response are greatly influenced by the gut microbiota. Mood disorders, including sadness and inflammation, have been connected. An unbalanced microbiota might result in persistent low-level inflammation, which may have an impact on mood and general emotional health.

Short-Chain Fatty Acids: Short-chain fatty acids (SCFAs), including butyrate, are produced and broken down by gut bactcria. SCFAs are recognized for their ability to reduce inflammation and for their part in preserving a healthy gut lining. A microbiome that is out of balance may produce less SCFA, which might have an impact on mood and cognitive ability.

The reaction to stress The gut microbiota may have an impact on how the body handles stress. According to studies, a balanced microbiome may help control the body's stress response and even foster emotions of peace.

The gut-brain axis Through a bidirectional network referred to as the "gut-brain axis," the gut and the brain can interact. This link enables information to go from the stomach to the brain, affecting mood, emotions and even cognitive performance. This communication may be hampered by a microbiome that is out of balance, which may have an impact on mental health.

It's important to understand that although there is mounting evidence of the gut-brain link and the gut microbiome's function in mood regulation, additional study is still needed to fully understand these connections. Diet, lifestyle, and individual differences are all variables that may affect how the gut flora affects mood. As microbiome research develops, it could provide new insights into methods for fostering emotional stability and mental health, perhaps via dietary and lifestyle changes that promote a balanced gut microbiota.

CHAPTER TWO

PTSD AND GUT MEMORY:

Restoring emotional health

A stressful occurrence might cause a person to suffer or witness post-traumatic stress disorder (PTSD), a mental health condition. Anyone who has experienced a traumatic incident, such as a battle, a natural catastrophe, sexual assault, a vehicle accident, or any other occurrence that generates acute anxiety, helplessness, or terror, may develop post-traumatic stress disorder (PTSD). Flashbacks, nightmares, extreme anxiety, and uncontrolled thoughts connected to the traumatic incident are some typical PTSD symptoms. Additionally, it may cause modifications to cognition, memory, and mood.

A relatively recent field of study called "gut memory" looks at the relationship between the stomach and the brain. It falls within the larger category of the gut-brain axis. The bulk of research has been on how gut microbiota affects mood, behavior, and mental health; nevertheless, the concept of gut memory is still poorly understood and is a relatively new area of study.

Researchers have discovered that the vagus nerve and the release of signaling molecules are two of the many channels by which the gut interacts with the brain. The collection of microbes in the gastrointestinal tract, known as the gut microbiome, contributes to this communication. The gut microbiota may affect memory, emotion, and behavior by creating neurotransmitters and other signaling molecules, according to recent studies. There is little information on the precise connection between gut memory and PTSD in this circumstance. However, some research has looked at how the gut microbiota may affect memory and cognition in stress-related circumstances.

The gut microbiota and gut memory may have a connection to disorders like PTSD, but additional study is required to properly understand this. Research is underway to better understand the gut-brain connection's involvement in memory, emotions, and mental health. It is a dynamic and complicated system. When treating

PTSD and other similar problems, it's crucial to seek the advice of medical specialists. It is a challenging and developing field of study to restore emotional wellness in the setting of PTSD and the possible contribution of gut memory. While knowledge of these relationships is still developing, there are many activities and tactics that may help PTSD sufferers feel emotional well:

1. Counseling and therapy PTSD may be effectively treated with psychotherapy, especially trauma-focused treatments like

cognitive behavioral therapy (CBT) and eye movement desensitization and reprocessing (EMDR). Therapy aids in the processing of painful memories and the development of coping mechanisms.

2. Medications A medical expert may sometimes recommend medication to treat PTSD symptoms, including sadness, anxiety, or sleep problems. These drugs may aid with mood regulation and enhance general emotional health.

3. Stress Management Techniques: Deep breathing exercises, yoga, meditation, and

other relaxation methods may all be used to reduce stress and anxiety. These techniques could indirectly improve emotional well-being and the gut-brain axis.

4. Do this exercise. It has been shown that regular exercise is beneficial for one's mental and emotional well-being. Exercise may boost happiness by releasing endorphins, which are feel-good chemicals that can lower stress.

5. Balanced Diet: Both physical and mental health may be supported by a nutritious and

balanced diet. Consuming nutrients like fiber-rich meals, fruits, vegetables, and probiotics that support a varied and healthy gut flora may indirectly improve general well-being.

6. Prebiotics and probiotics Some people discover that prebiotic-rich meals (which feed healthy gut flora) and probiotic pills or foods containing live cultures boost their mental well-being. These could be worth taking into account when working with a healthcare professional, while research in this field is still underway.

7. Getting enough sleep: Sleeping well is essential for emotional well-being. Good sleep hygiene, having a pleasant resting environment, and keeping a regular sleep pattern all contribute to overall well-being.

8. Social Assistance: A robust social network of family and friends may provide emotional support and a sense of community, both of which are crucial for emotional well-being.

9. Self-care and education Learning about PTSD and its conceivable connections to the

gut microbiota might enable people to make wise decisions about their health. Setting boundaries, controlling stress, and engaging in self-compassion exercises are all important self-care techniques.

10. Seek the Advice of a Healthcare Professional: It is crucial to seek advice from mental health experts and healthcare providers who can provide personalized therapy and support if you are coping with emotional health issues associated with PTSD.

Although there is growing interest in the idea of gut memory in the context of PTSD, therapeutic applications are still being developed. Therefore, evidence-based therapy, medical treatments, and holistic well-being practices continue to be the main methods for helping people with PTSD regain their emotional health. Further understanding of the gut-brain link may open up new treatment and support options in the future as research in this area continues.

CHAPTER THREE

THE HORMONES ROLE

Finding the Connection of the gut-mood

The endocrine system and hormones interact in a variety of ways with the gut microbiome, which is made up of billions of bacteria living in the gastrointestinal tract. This intricate link affects the immune system, emotions, and even metabolism to affect health and homeostasis. As they relate to the gut microbiota, hormones have several functions, including the following:

1. Appetite and Metabolism Amphetamine intake and body weight are controlled by hormones like leptin and ghrelin. As a signal to the brain that the body has ample energy reserves, leptin, which is generated by fat cells, suppresses hunger. Hunger is induced by ghrelin, which is generated in the stomach. The gut microbiota may affect these hormones, which in turn can affect appetite and energy metabolism. Because these hormonal signals are impacted by the gut flora, obesity, and weight gain may result.

2. inflammatory response: The gut microbiota is important in immune system regulation, and the gut-brain axis may affect the levels of hormones like cortisol, an anti-inflammatory hormone. The gut microbiota may experience dysbiosis, which can worsen inflammation. Chronic inflammation is linked to several disorders, including inflammatory bowel disease and metabolic syndrome.

3. Mood and Stress Response: Hormonal signaling is involved in the gut-brain axis,

which links the central nervous system with the gastrointestinal tract. Both the stomach and the brain create hormones that regulate mood, including serotonin, dopamine, and norepinephrine. These hormones may be influenced by gut microbiota imbalances, which may impact mood and stress responses.

4. Insulin Sensitivity A crucial factor in controlling blood sugar levels is insulin sensitivity, which the gut flora may affect. In the control of blood sugar, hormones like glucagon and insulin are important. Insulin

resistance, a risk factor for type 2 diabetes, may be exacerbated by poor gut flora.

5. The Role of the Immune System In addition to the gut microbiome's crucial function in teaching the immune system, hormones may affect immunological responses. This equilibrium may be upset by dysbiosis, which might result in autoimmune diseases and inflammatory reactions.

6. Nutritional Metabolic Rate: The gut flora may impact food absorption and utilization,

and hormones like thyroid hormones can alter metabolism. The control of hormones and general health may be impacted by dysbiosis in the gut, which may interfere with these procedures.

It's important to remember that research in this area is still ongoing, and the specific processes by which the gut microbiota and hormones interact are currently being investigated.

Nonetheless, it is evident that the gut microbiota and hormones have a dynamic interaction, and maintaining a healthy gut microbiome is crucial for general well-being and hormone control. The gut microbiota may be supported, and the functions associated with hormones can be regulated with the use of prebiotics, probiotics, and a healthy lifestyle. The body's endocrine system, a sophisticated network of glands, produces hormones, which are chemical messengers. They are crucial in the control of many physiological processes, the preservation of homeostasis, and the modification of mood and behavior. To have an impact on target cells and tissues, hormones must attach to particular receptors in those cells and tissues before being discharged into the circulation. The following are some of the main functions that hormones serve in the body:

1. Metabolism regulation To control blood sugar levels, hormones such as insulin and glucagon are used. Glucagon increases blood sugar levels by encouraging the liver's release of glucose, while insulin makes it easier for cells to absorb glucose.

2. Development and Growth: Growth hormone, a hormone produced by the

pituitary gland, is essential for a child's development. The development of secondary sexual traits throughout puberty is also influenced by sex hormones like estrogen and testosterone.

3. The ability to reproduce Female menstrual cycles and male sperm production are both regulated by hormones. These include luteinizing hormone (LH), estrogen, progesterone, and follicle-stimulating hormone (FSH).

4. In reaction to stress, the adrenal glands produce epinephrine and other chemicals like cortisol. These hormones set off the "fight or flight" reaction, speeding up the heart rate and getting the body ready to defend itself against an impending danger.

5. Control of the Thyroid: Thyroxine (T4) and triiodothyronine (T3), the thyroid gland's main hormones, are produced and have an impact on energy generation, metabolism, and body temperature.

6. Calcium Regulation: The body's calcium levels are regulated by the parathyroid hormone (PTH) and calcitonin, which also help to keep muscles, nerves, and bones healthy.

7. Fluid-Electrolyte Balance: Antidiuretic hormone (ADH) and other hormones like aldosterone assist in keeping the body's water and electrolyte balance in check.

8. Immune System Function Cytokines and other immune system hormones control the body's immunological response, which

includes inflammation and infection protection.

9. Mood and behavior: A person's mood, conduct, and emotions may be affected by hormones. There are three neurotransmitter hormones linked to mood regulation: serotonin, dopamine, and norepinephrine.

10. The pineal gland's release of melatonin, which aids in the regulation of the sleep-wake cycle and circadian rhythms, causes the sleep-wake cycle to occur.

11. Appetite Regulation: Hormones like ghrelin and leptin help control hunger and weight.

12. Pregnancy and nursing: Hormones such as progesterone, estrogen, and human chorionic gonadotropin (hCG) aid embryonic development throughout pregnancy. Prolactin and oxytocin are hormones that govern breastfeeding and maternal bonding after delivery.

13. Aging: As people get older, their levels of hormones, including growth hormone,

estrogen, and testosterone, decrease, which causes the body to alter with age.

The body's hormones must be kept in balance if it is to be healthy and happy generally. Hormone imbalances may need medical treatment and hormone replacement therapy and may result in several health problems. Specialists in the endocrine system known as endocrinologists diagnose and treat conditions linked to hormones.

It's a challenging and dynamic area of study to study how the stomach affects mood. There are numerous techniques to investigate and comprehend the gut-mood relationship, even though the particular processes are not entirely understood. They are as follows:

1. Keep a food and mood diary. Begin by recording your eating habits and emotional state in a journal. You may find trends and possible triggers by doing this. Be mindful of how certain meals or dietary practices may influence your mood.

2. Think About Dietary Modifications: Consider making moderate dietary changes to see if they affect your mood. Consider increasing your consumption of probiotics, prebiotics, and fiber-rich meals as examples of foods that will help your body. These foods will all help your body by feeding the good bacteria in your gut. It could also be advantageous to cut back on highly processed or sugary meals.

3. Mindfulness While Eating Use mindful eating to your advantage by focusing

entirely on the sensory aspects of your meal. Your awareness of how various meals affect your physical and mental well-being might improve as a result.

4. Managing Stress: The gut microbiota and mood may both be harmed by prolonged stress. Learn how to handle stress and how it affects your gut and mood by practicing stress-reduction strategies like yoga, progressive muscle relaxation, deep breathing, meditation, or deep breathing.

5. Seek Professional Guidance: If You Have Specific Concerns About Your Gut-Mood Connection, Consult with a Registered Dietitian or Healthcare Professional. Following your demands, they may provide individualized advice and suggest dietary changes or dietary supplements.

6. Understanding food sensitivities: Food sensitivities or allergies may harm mood in certain people. If you have any reason to believe this, you may want to discuss finding and managing any particular food triggers with a healthcare professional.

7. Supplements that include probiotics If you take probiotic supplements, talk about it with your doctor. Probiotic strains that have shown promise in mood control still need more study. However individual differences in the consequences may occur.

8. Preventatively avoid antibiotics: The equilibrium of the gut microbiota may be upset by overusing antibiotics. If your doctor has given antibiotics, be careful to take them as recommended, and think about taking a probiotic supplement to

maintain your gut health both throughout and after the course of treatment.

9. Maintain your knowledge. Keep up with new developments in the study of gut-brain connections. Knowing how these two things are related will help you make wise decisions about your nutrition and way of life. Discoveries are always being made.

10. Consult a medical specialist: Seeking advice from a medical expert, such as a gastroenterologist, psychiatrist, or integrative medicine specialist, is crucial if

you have recurrent mood disorders or digestive problems. They can provide a thorough assessment and make therapy suggestions.

Please keep in mind that the gut-mood relationship is very idiosyncratic and that what works for one person may not work for another. Because of this, it's crucial to explore this link slowly and be open to making little adjustments as you become more aware of how your body reacts to various food and lifestyle options.

CHAPTER FOUR

FREE FROM ANXIETY

enhancing social competence and controlling the inner storm

Take, for example, releasing your anxieties Even though it is the end of the workday, your supervisor is still pressing you to finish a paper. You start crying out loud or finding it difficult to breathe all of a sudden. If the kids start fighting again, you may lose your cool and shout at them to stop. Then, right away, you may start beating yourself up for your outburst. Because you are unsure of how to handle these emotions, you often choose to bury them or shove them away by choosing an unhealthy diversion. Please know that you are not alone if this sounds similar. That's simply a characteristic of being human; we all sometimes deal with intense emotional responses. The inability to control one's emotions in healthy, productive ways, however, may be a chronic issue for some individuals, which can have some unfavorable effects. Emotions may be valuable when used in the appropriate proportions. They enlighten us, sway our judgment, and force us to take action. For instance, if you are afraid when alone at night and you hear footsteps, your brain will quickly mobilize you to prepare to flee if there is a threat. Alternately, if you feel like you're being treated unfairly, you'll be inspired to act differently to influence how others treat you. The truth is that feelings may hurt and be upsetting. We work to control and overcome them when they come up. This process, known as emotion regulation, may include diverting our focus away from the source of our suffering, altering our perspective of the circumstance, or altering our behavior. Emotion regulation aids in calming our feelings so they are easier to control, but it does not (and shouldn't) make them completely go away. When our ability to control our emotions in a healthy, productive manner is compromised by overpowering emotions, problems result. Emotion dysregulation is the term for this. Everybody sometimes experiences dysregulation, especially when we are coping with extraordinary events like a pandemic, a natural catastrophe, or the loss of a loved one. But when it happens often, even in response to modest stress, it may lead to pandemonium. It makes it difficult for a person to function in daily life and is a contributing factor to a wide range of mental health issues, including mood and anxiety disorders. Dysregulation also plays a role in self-harm and suicidality, and it motivates harmful behaviors including drug misuse, disordered eating, and other ways of escaping difficult feelings and ideas. When they are growing up, the majority of individuals learn how to control their emotions. However, some people's coping mechanisms are harmful or ineffective. The biosocial hypothesis from dialectical behavior therapy (DBT), a kind of therapy, is one idea explaining why this occurs. Following this theory, some people are born with a higher level of emotional sensitivity, which causes them to react emotionally to things more strongly, take longer to get over those intense feelings, and generally experience more emotional pain (such as more anger, sadness, shame, or anxiety). This emotional sensitivity (the "bio" component of the theory) is not unusual and is not a problem in and of itself, but when we combine this with a problematic environment (i.e., the "social" half), things may become complicated. Particularly, some kids develop in a setting where they constantly feel rejected. Their emotions, ideas, and bodily feelings are often punished or disregarded, and they frequently hear that there is something wrong with them. We have the ideal storm that leads to emotion dysregulation when a kid who is very sensitive to emotional cues is raised in a setting where they are often invalidated. Borderline personality disorder, which is characterized by intense, persistent emotion dysregulation and a propensity for suicidal and self-destructive behavior, was the initial target of DBT, which was developed by American psychologist Marsha Linehan. To help individuals better control their emotions, DBT focuses on giving them the skills they need. For many additional mental health issues, such as depression and anxiety disorders, many therapists now use a DBT-informed therapy strategy. No matter the issues my clients are facing, I teach DBT methods to all of them as a psychotherapist. This manual explains how to navigate and control intense emotions using DBT techniques. Core mindfulness skills, distress tolerance skills, emotion regulation skills, and interpersonal effectiveness skills are the four sets of skills taught in DBT. These skills help people live more in the present moment and adopt an accepting, open mindset toward their experience, while distress tolerance skills help people navigate crises without making them worse. The first three abilities will be the main emphasis of this guide.

For more than 20 years, I've provided mental health services to people with a range of issues. I've seen firsthand the effectiveness of DBT and used many of the techniques. I want to give you some tips from many courses that will enable you to better manage your emotions both immediately and over the long term, even if we are unable to cover all the abilities in depth at this time. Steps to take the first thing you should focus on is becoming re-regulated as soon as you can, since when emotions are already high, it might be difficult to think about how you can assist yourself. Here are a few quick techniques that alter your body's chemistry. It will be most beneficial if you practice them before you're in a stressful scenario so you know how to apply them.To re-regulate, try these easy fixes.One of my favorite re-regulating techniques is to bend forward. No matter whether you can truly touch your toes, crouch down as if you were attempting to do so. If necessary, you may even do this while seated by placing your head between your knees. Spend a few seconds there (30 to 60 seconds, if you can) and take a few calm, deep breaths. Making a forward bend stimulates our parasympathetic nervous system, often known as our "rest and digest" system, which promotes a sense of calm and helps us slow down. When you're ready to get up again, just take your time. You don't want to trip over yourself. It may seem cliche, but breathing is one of the greatest methods to bring your emotions down to a more bearable level. Concentrate on your exhale while practicing "paced breathing." To help yourself feel a bit calmer and bring your emotions down to a more bearable level, concentrate, in particular, on making your exhale longer than your inhale. This engages our parasympathetic nervous system. When you inhale, mentally calculate the length of your breath; when you exhale, do the same, making sure your exhale is at least a tiny bit longer than your inhale. For instance, if you inhale to 4, make sure you exhale to at least 5. Combine this breathing with a forward bend for a double-whammy. Your emotions will start to strengthen again if nothing else changes in your surroundings; therefore, the following stages are also necessary. These re-regulating abilities will aid in your ability to think more clearly for a short period. Increase your emotional awareness. Long-term emotional management requires a greater understanding of your emotions and all of their components, as well as the ability to identify them appropriately. It may seem weird to say this since, after all, you are aware of your feelings. But how can you tell whether what you've always referred to as "anger" is anger and not just anxiety? The majority of us just believe that what we think we feel is what we truly feel, much like how we assume the color we've always named "blue" is indeed blue, but how can we know? Sensitive people who have grown up in a pervasively invalidating environment often learn to disregard or not believe their emotional experiences, as well as attempt to avoid or escape those feelings, which makes it harder for them to appropriately name emotions. Anyone prone to emotion dysregulation may find it difficult to identify their emotions, leading them to suffuse their surroundings with an emotional "fog." Do you know what emotion you're experiencing when you say you're "upset," "bad," or "off"? The next time you feel even a slight feeling, if you have trouble controlling it, think about each of the following questions: What was the motivating circumstance or feeling's catalyst? What caused you to respond? (Simply be descriptive; don't assess if your answer was correct or incorrect.)What did you think of the predicament? How did you perceive what was occurring? Did you catch yourself passing judgment, drawing conclusions too quickly, or making assumptions? What changes in your physique did you notice? What about stiffness or tension in certain areas? breathing, heartbeat, or body temperature changes? Your body was doing what? Describe your posture, facial expression, and body language. What impulses did you observe? Want to scream or throw things? To avoid or get out of a situation, did you feel the impulse to avoid eye contact? Which actions did you take? Have any of the impulses you listed above been acted upon? Did you substitute another action? You will be able to appropriately identify your feelings more often after completing this practice. After asking yourself the above questions, you may try determining if your feelings fall into one of the following four (nearly rhymes) categories: angry, sad, joyful, or fearful. These are the terms I use with clients to help differentiate between fundamental emotions, but you may progressively work on being more precise; emotion lists can also be useful. Why is this significant, you may be thinking? However, if you can't identify it, you can't control it, according to American psychiatrist Dan Siegel. Once you can recognize your emotions, you'll be better equipped to decide what to do about them. The first step is to validate the emotion you're feeling, which is the second skill we'll look at in this article.

Anxiety is a typical and normal reaction to stress or perceived dangers, but when it persists or gets out of control, it may negatively affect your health. The following techniques may be used to control and lessen anxiety:

- Deep-breathing exercises and relaxation methods: Engage in deep breathing techniques to relax your body. Breathe in deeply for a count of 4, hold your breath for a count of 4, and then let out slowly for a count of 4. Repeat. Try progressive muscle relaxation, when each muscle group in your body is tensed and then relaxed. This may aid in easing anxiety-related bodily tension.

- Exercise Regularly: Exercise, including brisk walking, running, or yoga, helps lower anxiety by producing endorphins, which are organic mood enhancers.

- Healthy Diet: Steer clear of excessive amounts of coffee and sweets, which may heighten anxiety. Consider a balanced diet that includes whole foods, fruits, vegetables, and lean meats instead. Because magnesium may have a soothing impact, take into account foods high in magnesium, such as leafy greens, nuts, and seeds.

- Get adequate, quality sleep. Be careful to get adequate rest. Lack of sleep may make anxiety worse.

- Mindfulness and meditation: You can remain in the now and lessen worry by regularly practicing mindfulness and meditation. You may find instructions for these techniques in apps and on online sites.

- Limit Exposure to Stressors: Determine the causes of stress and anxiety in your life and devise tactics to minimize or completely avoid them.

- Professional treatment: If anxiety is seriously interfering with your everyday life, think about getting treatment from a mental health expert, such as a therapist, counselor, or psychiatrist. They are able to provide counseling, treatment, and, if required, medication.

- Cognitive behavioral therapy (CBT): CBT is an evidence-based treatment technique that aids people in recognizing and altering unfavorable thinking patterns and actions that fuel worry.

- Social Support: Discuss your anxiety with friends and family. Sometimes, simply talking about your emotions may be therapeutic. In order to manage anxiety, having a support system might be essential.

- Set realistic goals: refrain from giving oneself too many obligations. Prioritize self-care and set attainable objectives.

- Mindful Time Management: Manage your time well to avoid stress caused by procrastination or overcommitting.

- "Limit Exposure to Anxiety Triggers": Recognize the circumstances, persons, or surroundings that make you anxious. Limit your exposure to these triggers whenever you can.

- Refrain from using alcohol and other drugs since they might make anxiety worse and aggravate other mental health conditions.

- Self-Care: Schedule time for relaxing and enjoyable self-care pursuits, including hobbies, reading, and time spent in nature.

- Journaling: Putting your ideas and emotions into writing will help you put your worries into perspective and keep tabs on your development.

Your interpersonal interactions and general well-being may be considerably enhanced by improving your social skills and managing your internal emotional turbulence. You may use the following tactics to aid you on your journey:

- Self-awareness: recognize and comprehend your feelings and emotional causes. The first step in managing your inner emotional tempest is being self-aware.

- Emotion Regulation: Develop excellent emotional management skills. You may maintain your composure and calm in difficult times by using techniques like deep breathing, mindfulness, and meditation.

- Empathy: Try to comprehend others' feelings and points of view in order to demonstrate empathy. This might enable you to react sympathetically and thoughtfully.

- Active Listening: Give them your complete attention to improve your listening abilities. To be sure you comprehend their wants and emotions, listen without passing judgment, and provide clarifying questions.

- Communication Skills: Improve your ability to communicate clearly and forcefully. Thoughts and sentiments should be expressed openly and with respect. Stay away from confrontational or passive-aggressive language.

- Conflict Resolution: Acquire good conflict management and resolution skills. Instead of concentrating on "winning" fights, try to discover solutions that benefit all parties.

- Practice stress-reduction strategies in order to calm down emotional turbulence. This involves time management, meditation, exercise, and relaxation.

- Seek Support: When necessary, get in touch with friends, relatives, or a therapist. Talking about your feelings might help you gain important perspective and experience emotional relief.

- Mindfulness: Use mindfulness exercises to maintain present-moment awareness. This may assist you in avoiding emotional responses that result from unpleasant memories or anxiety about the future.

- Patience: Practice patience with both yourself and other people. It takes time and effort to master emotional regulation and social intelligence.

- Self-Care: Make self-care a priority by getting enough sleep, eating healthy food, and doing things that make you happy and calm you, and establish sound limits in your interactions.

- Setting limits: Recognize your comfort zone and express your limits in a straightforward manner. The use of positive affirmations may help you question unhelpful thinking patterns and swap them out for healthy, self-affirming ideas.

- Reflect on what you've learned: Consider what you learned from the event and how you might improve your answers going forward after challenging social or emotional circumstances.

- Education: Read books or enroll in classes on effective communication and emotional intelligence. Your social skills may improve with ongoing study.

Keep in mind that developing social skills and emotional self-control are continual processes. It's crucial to practice these skills often and have patience with yourself. You may develop a better sense of how to handle social situations and keep your emotions in check over time.

CHAPTER FIVE

RESTORATION

Improving gut health may improve sleep and emotional well-being.

Manipulating gut bacteria in the microbiome, through the use of probiotics and prebiotics, has been found to influence both physical and emotional well-being. This study uses a dietary manipulation 'The Gut Makeover' designed to elicit positive changes to the gut bacteria within the microbiome. 21 healthy participants undertook 'The Gut Makeover' for a four-week period. Weight and various aspects of health were assessed pre and post intervention using the Functional Medicine Medical Symptoms Questionnaire (MSQ). Paired sample t-tests revealed a significant reduction in self-reported weight at the end of the intervention. Adverse medical symptoms related to digestion, cognition, and physical and emotional well-being, were also significantly reduced during the course of the dietary intervention. The intervention, designed to manipulate gut bacteria, had a significant impact on digestion, reducing IBS-type symptoms in this non-clinical population. There was also a striking reduction in negative symptoms related to cognition, memory, and emotional well-being, including symptoms of anxiety and depression. Dietary gut microbiome manipulations may have the power to exert positive physical and psychological health benefits, of a similar nature to those reported in studies using pre- and probiotics. The small sample size and lack of control over confounding variables mean that it will be important to replicate these findings in larger-scale controlled, prospective, clinical trials. This dietary microbiome intervention has the potential to improve physical and emotional well-being in the general population but also to be investigated as a treatment option for individuals with conditions as diverse as IBS, anxiety, depression, and Alzheimer's disease.

Why does our gut matter?

There are three main reasons why we need to think about our gut health. Firstly, our intestinal tract (bowel) contains trillions of microbes. These are a hugely important part of our health: they produce different hormones and vitamins, and we couldn't survive without them.

Secondly, the majority of the cells that make up our immune system are found in our digestive tract. Having good gut health is linked to fewer sick days and a lower risk of allergies and autoimmune conditions. Finally, even if you put the healthiest food into your body, if you don't have a healthy intestinal lining to digest it, you won't get all the benefits of what you are eating.

How do I know if I have a healthy gut?

There is no single way to tell if you have a healthy gut – it's a collection of factors. Constipation, diarrhea, or stomach cramps can be signs of an unhealthy gut. But just because you don't notice any symptoms, it doesn't mean you have good gut health. Other factors include:

how often you get sick

whether you are on a restrictive diet

what medications you take

What can I do to have a healthier gut?

Diet is one of the biggest influences on our gut health, because our microbes are reliant on what we feed them. This explains why even identcal twins (who will have identical genetics) have different microbes. Things like sleep, stress, and exercise can also change the microbes, so it's important to look at your lifestyle.

What should I eat to help my gut health?
One of the strategies I recommend is to eat 30 different plant foods every week. Diversity matters, because there are nearly

100 types of fiber and thousands of plant phytochemicals, which are thought to feed different bacteria. Thirty might sound intimidating, but it includes fruits and vegetables, whole grains, legumes (such as chickpeas, lentils, or kidney beans), nuts, and seeds. It could be as simple as adding mixed seeds to whatever you are eating in the morning.

Make small switches, such as buying different colors of peppers instead of a single one, or a pack of mixed vegetables. Don't try to have the same meals every day.

Even if you love routine, have different fruit on different days, or if you eat porridge every day, vary the toppings – banana one day, berries another, along with nuts and seeds.

To improve general health and well-being, the gut flora must be balanced again. A range of health problems may result from a disruption in the gut's delicate balance of helpful and dangerous bacteria. The following techniques may be used to get the gut microbiota back in balance:

1. Dietary Changes: Eat a variety of fiber-rich foods such as fruits, vegetables, whole grains, and legumes. These provide the good bacteria in the stomach with nutrition to grow. Include fermented foods in your diet, such as kombucha, kimchi, yogurt, kefir, and sauerkraut. These meals include live probiotics, which may be able to assist your gut balance again.

Include foods high in prebiotics, such as garlic, onions, leeks, asparagus, and bananas, in your diet. Non-digestible fibers called prebiotics provide food for good bacteria in the stomach.

2.   Probiotic   Supplements: Take   into consideration using probiotic supplements, particularly if you just finished an antibiotic treatment or are experiencing digestive problems. For assistance in selecting the best probiotic for your needs, speak with a healthcare practitioner.

3. Limit your use of antibiotics by adhering to the recommended course of therapy and only taking them when necessary. The gut microbiota may be harmed by excessive use of antibiotics.

5. Reduce stress: The gut microbiota might suffer from long-term stress. Utilize methods that may help you manage your stress, such as yoga, meditation, and deep breathing exercises.

6. Get adequate, high-quality sleep; lack of sleep may have a negative impact on gut health.

7. Stay Hydrated: Drink a lot of water to promote digestion and have a healthy gut.

8. Exercise Regularly: Physical exercise, which has been demonstrated to have a favorable impact on the gut flora, should be done on a regular basis.

9. Avoid Too Much Sugar and Processed Foods: High sugar and processed food consumption might be harmful to gut health. Don't eat as much of them.

10. Stay Hydrated: Getting enough amounts of water is essential for keeping the stomach in good shape and allowing nutrients to flow around freely.

11. Appropriate Chewing: Chewing your meal completely promotes digestion and improves nutrition absorption in the stomach.

12. Digestive Enzymes: To aid in digestion and nutrition absorption, some people may profit from taking supplements of digestive enzymes.

13. Consult a Healthcare Professional: Consult a gastroenterologist or healthcare professional for a comprehensive assessment and individualized advice if you

have persistent digestive problems or believe your gut microbiota is seriously out of balance.

CHAPTER SIX

EMOTIONAL WELL-BEING ACROSS LIFE'S STAGES

Promoting it from early childhood to the halcyon years

"Gut health across the lifespan" refers to the value of preserving a healthy gastrointestinal tract from early childhood to old age. Our health and wellbeing depend heavily on the function of the gut, also referred to as the gastrointestinal tract. This idea acknowledges that gut health should be considered throughout one's life rather than being a worry just for a certain age group. It consists of the following:

It is vital to start life with a balanced gut microbiota. One way to assist in the development of a good gut is through breastfeeding, which offers necessary nutrients and healthy bacteria. Long-term intestinal health may be influenced by early eating choices.

As kids get older, their diets change. To support a varied and healthy gut microbiota, it's crucial to maintain a balanced and nutritious diet. Currently, the condition of the gut may affect growth, development, and general health.

For proper digestion, nutrition absorption, and general health in adulthood, one must have a healthy gut. The gut microbiota may be disturbed by poor diet, stress, and certain drugs. It's important to have a healthy diet while also controlling your stress.

For both the mother and the growing child, a healthy gut throughout pregnancy is crucial. Throughout pregnancy and the reproductive years, changes in immune function and hormone levels may have an impact on gut health.

Changes in gut microbes are among the changes that aging may bring about. For the body to absorb nutrients and function properly, older individuals must maintain good gut health. A specialized probiotic supplement and dietary modifications may be necessary to accommodate aging-related changes.

Digestion problems, metabolic syndrome, and autoimmune illnesses are just a few of the ailments that a healthy gut may help to avoid. A healthy stomach may help lower the chance of developing certain diseases throughout life. Immune function and intestinal health are intimately related. Every stage of life benefits from a healthy gut microbiota that supports a strong immune system. An association between intestinal health and mood has been shown in a recent study. Consideration should be given to gut health at all stages of life since it may improve mental health.

Throughout life, encouraging gut health may help people live longer and age in a healthy way. Age-related disorders may be prevented by maintaining a healthy gut flora. Maintaining good gut health may be especially important for those with chronic health issues. Irritable bowel syndrome (IBS) and inflammatory bowel disease (IBD) are two chronic illnesses that have a direct impact on the digestive system.

In conclusion, "gut health across the lifespan" underlines how crucial it is to maintain a healthy gut microbiota from infancy to old age. This idea emphasizes the link between gut health and general well-being and motivates people to spend their lives making decisions that promote their gut health.

In the book Nurturing Emotional Well-Being from Infancy to Brighter Years, the importance of fostering emotional well-being and resilience is emphasized across all phases of life, from early infancy to older adulthood. It emphasizes the notion that emotional health is not static but rather develops over time and may be fostered and enhanced throughout one's existence. Here is a description of what this idea entails:

Early childhood does contribute to emotional well-being, which starts in infancy. The emotional ties that babies form with their caretakers create the groundwork for all future interactions. Early emotional development requires a secure, adoring, and responsive environment.

As kids get older, they encounter a variety of emotions and learn how to deal with them. It's crucial to develop emotional intelligence, which involves knowing how to recognize and control emotions. In order to foster mental health throughout these early years, parents and educators are crucial.

Throughout maturity, emotional health continues to change. People deal with a variety of life obstacles, such as changing careers, navigating relationships, and becoming parents. The ability to cope with these difficulties while maintaining emotional stability is essential.

At any age, having healthy connections is essential for emotional wellbeing. Fostering wholesome and encouraging relationships, whether they be with friends, family, or love partners, benefits emotional well-being.

In order to effectively manage stress, hardship, and life changes, coping skills must be developed. People may acquire techniques like problem-solving, mindfulness, and reaching out for social support to improve their emotional resiliency.

Understanding one's mental health and getting assistance when necessary are crucial. An essential component of fostering emotional well-being is eradicating the stigma associated with mental health concerns.

For emotional well-being, stress management is essential. Emotional resilience may be improved by putting stress-reduction practices like exercise, meditation, and time management into practice. Strengths, wellbeing, and happiness are the main topics of positive psychology. People may have a more upbeat and cheerful attitude toward life by using positive psychology concepts.

Maintaining social relationships, adjusting to retirement, and dealing with the emotional effects of aging, such as loss and grieving, are all necessary for the emotional well-being of older adults. Throughout their lives, people may evaluate their level of life satisfaction and make adjustments to better balance their objectives, values, and emotional well-being.

CONCLUSION

I will finish by emphasizing that the process of promoting emotional well-being during a lifetime is dynamic and ever-changing. The theory highlights the significance of emotional well-being at every stage of life, from the fragile moments of infancy to the joyful years of elder adulthood. Through this approach, individuals may increase their emotional intelligence, establish solid coping strategies, and foster healthy relationships. To enhance their well-being, people may develop coping methods for dealing with stress, seek support when they need it, and embrace positive psychological beliefs. The notion also underlines how vital it is to cope with mental health issues, eliminate stigma, and keep a sense of enjoyment in life. Nurturing emotional well-being is a lifelong commitment to one's own growth and happiness, whether it requires relaxing an infant, supporting a child's emotional development, or confronting the obstacles of maturity and aging. As individuals learn to embrace their feelings, build on their strengths, and foster lasting happiness, the path to emotional well-being ultimately stands as a testimony to the power of the human spirit. It opens up the prospect of a life that is better and more emotionally rewarding.

Description

In a world where understanding the value of holistic health is growing, "Mental Well-Being and Digestive Process" takes you on an investigation into the fundamental relationship that exists between your mind and stomach. This book serves as a guide to help you comprehend how your entire health may be significantly impacted by the complex interactions between digestive and mental health. Explore the intriguing realm of the gut-brain axis, where your mood, emotions, and cognitive function may all be impacted by the delicate balance of microbes, nutrients, and neurological impulses that affect your digestive system. This book breaks down the riddles of how eating habits might impact emotions through an analysis of the most recent scientific studies and professional perspectives. Learn doable tactics and dietary recommendations to support your mental wellness and improve your digestive health. This book gives a thorough method for improving both your physical and mental health, covering everything from the role that probiotics and diet play in fostering emotional resilience to the ways that stress and lifestyle decisions may affect your gut and mental health. "Mental Well-Being and Digestive Process" is your manual for attaining a balanced, healthy condition whereby digestive harmony leads to a life that is happier and more fulfilled. Discover how to use your gut's ability to support mental health and set out on a path to improved physical and emotional balance.

keyword
health
gut health for women
book leaky
by-health
guts
for the women